CORPORATE DESIGN SYSTEMS

2

Identity Through Graphics

Motoo Nakanishi, and The CoCoMAS Committee

PBC International, Inc. ■ New York

Distributors to the trade in the United States:

Robert Silver Associates
95 Madison Avenue
New York, NY 10016

Distributors to the trade in Canada:

General Publishing Co. Ltd.
30 Lesmill Road
Don Mills, Ontario, Canada M3B 2T6

Distributed in Continental Europe by:

Feffer and Simons, B.V.
170 Rijnkade
Weesp, Netherlands

Distributed throughout the rest of the world by:

Fleetbooks, S.A.
℅ Feffer and Simons, Inc.
100 Park Avenue
New York, NY 10017

Library of Congress Cataloging in Publication Data

Nakanishi, Motoo, 1938–
   Corporate design.

   1. Corporate image.   2. Logotype.   I. Title.
HD59.2.N35   1984   658.8'27   84-22778
ISBN 0-86636-004-2

The first book in this series,
CORPORATE DESIGN SYSTEMS 1,
is available from:

   Art Direction Book Co.
   10 E. 39th Street
   New York, NY 10017

Printed in Hong Kong
by Toppan Printing Co. (H.K.) Ltd., Hong Kong

10 9 8 7 6 5 4 3 2 1

FOREWORD

"From DECOMAS to CoCoMAS"—this is the slogan we have coined to describe our theme of study.

One of the major themes confronting corporations within modern industrial society is that of communication. In recent years, the subject of corporate communication has been widely discussed and much attention given to the informational meaning of the corporation, its activities and products.

In 1964, we put out a book entitled "Design Policy" (Hamaguchi, R. and Nakanishi, M., Bijutsu Shuppan), followed in 1971 by "DECOMAS—Design Coordination as a Management Strategy" (ed. the DECOMAS Committee, Sanseido) in an attempt to share the fruits of our study, the core of which lies in the problems of corporations and design, as well as communication.

The object of our ten year study has been design, not of individual products or advertisements but that of design systems as part of a corporation's management strategy.

Our emphasis was placed on exploring the territorial problems that exist between design and marketing, or design and management within enterprises regardless of category or size. As an extension of this study we have also been examining the increasingly active role that corporations play in cultural aspects. The concern over communication today involves the problem of creating something worthy of communicating rather than simply the problems of design, medium, and methods to be exploited for communication.

From these numerous themes, we have focused on corporate design systems and are planning to publish fifteen or so volumes in four series. We believe that this series, when completed will serve as a precious record and data of design in the light of corporate management today. Fortunately, over the past ten years the informative materials we have continued to accumulate have become one of the world's largest collections.

We have developed our ideas and methodology in this field, and have also taken into consideration the objectives of readers in preparing this serialized publication.

We have named this series "from DECOMAS" as we firmly believe that design systems must be established as the basis of corporate communication activities. We are conscious that with the coming of the "communication-oriented age," the establishment of design systems is the starting point for CoCoMAS (Corporate Communication as a Management Strategy).

Furthermore, we have been privileged by the cooperation of many persons and corporations whose names will appear in each volume as an expression of our deepest appreciation.

On this occasion, I would especially like to extend my heartfelt gratitude to Messrs. N. Oda, T. Nakamura and Y. Mochizuki of the Creativity Development Center at SANNO Institute of Business Administration, to Mr. T. Hirota, ex-Director, Mr. K. Onozawa, Assistant Director and Mr. Y. Koizumi of the Publications Department of SANNO Institute of Business Administration who gave their advice and patient assistance in all aspects of this publication, to Miss H. Shudo, and to all our other friends.

Motoo Nakanishi, *Director,*
The CoCoMAS Committee

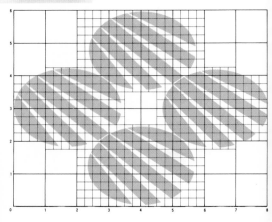

Deloitte
Haskins · Sells

Deloitte
Haskins · Sells
Chartered Accountants

Deloitte
Haskins · Sells   Management
                    Consultants Pty Ltd

Antonio
Leira Bastidas   Representantes de Deloitte Haskins & Sells

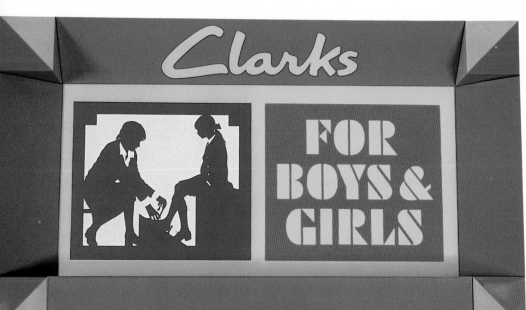

CONTENTS

Citibank	5
P&O	21
Deloitte Haskins & Sells	33
Watneys	43
Kenwood	55
Cummins	75
Clarks	85
The Citizens National Bank	97
Washington Zoo	111

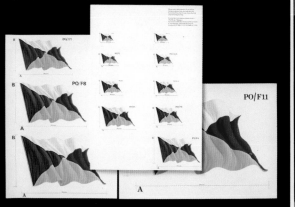

Citibank

Citibank, N.A.

Headquarters: New York, U.S.A.

Field of Business: Banking

Size of Organization: total assets/
    $130 billion
    number of employees/50,000

Design: Citibank- Anspach Grossman Portugal, Inc.
    (Eugene J. Grossman)
    Citicorp- Citibank Communications Design Dept.
    (Jack Odette, Vice President)

Year of First Implementation: 1976

1

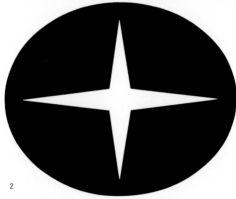

2

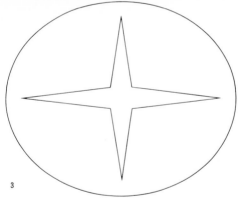

3

Citibank was founded in 1812 as the City Bank of New York and later came to be known as the First National City Bank of New York. Its creation of a holding company, Citicorp, in 1968, started a major trend among large banks as it allowed them to expand into areas previously forbidden to U.S. banks. Citibank's need for a corporate identity program arose from the complexity of its businesses and the fact that it was known by different names in many countries. As a result, the public was unaware that Citibank was one company.

Under the guidance of Citibank's Mr. Ed Dooley of Advertising and Marketing, and Mr. Jack Odette of Communication Design, the New York design firm of Anspach Grossman Portugal, Inc. created a new corporate identity program. The bank's name change to Citibank, N.A. was a integral part of the program announced in 1976. The uniqueness of the new

name differentiated the bank from others and gave it a consistent identity throughout the world. An advantage of the program is that Citibank is known as Citibank, eliminating the need for people to have to remember what a symbol stands for.

In 1981, the Communication Design Department extended the program to include a revitalized Citicorp program. Changes in the regulatory environment had allowed Citicorp to expand its business and it proved beneficial to use combined identifiers to reinforce each other.

1 Citibank Identifier as entrance sign
2·3 Symbol, solid and outline versions
4 Former symbol

4

5

CITIBANK✦

6

CITIBANK✦CITICORP

7

5 Citibank Identification Standards Manuals
6 The Citibank Identifier
   The logotype, followed by the symbol forms
   the identifier. The symbol may be used alone.
7 The Combined Identifier
   Use of this combined form is restricted by
   legal requirements. It may be used on signage
   at buildings occupied by both Citibank and a
   Citicorp subsidiary and as the identifier in
   advertising, when it speaks for both the bank
   and the corporation.
8 Citibank Identifier Colors
9 Unacceptable forms of the Citibank Iden-

tifier.
10 Reproduction materials
11 Citibank typefaces
   Helvetica is for stationery, forms, signs and
   institutional media. Other typefaces may be
   used for promotional matter.
12 Positioning of the identifier

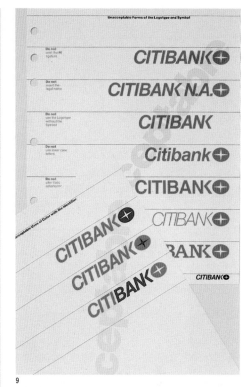

9

10

8

Helvetica Regular

ABCDEFGHIJKLMNOPQRSTUVWXYZ
abcdefghijklmnopqrstuvwxyz
1234567890 (&.,:;!?'"''-*$%/)

Helvetica Black

ABCDEFGHIJKLMNOPQRSTUVWXYZ
abcdefghijklmnopqrstuvwxyz
1234567890 (&.,:;!?'"''-*$%/)

Helvetica Regular Italic

ABCDEFGHIJKLMNOPQRSTUVWXYZ
abcdefghijklmonpqrstuvwxyz
1234567890(&.,:;!?'"''-$/)*

Baskerville
ABCDEFGHIJKLMNOPQRST
abcdefghijklmnopqrstuvwxyz
1234567890(&.,:;!?'"''-*$/)

Garamond
ABCDEFGHIJKLMNOPQRSTI
abcdefghijklmnopqrstuvwxyz
1234567890(&.,:;!?'"''-*$/)

Bodoni
ABCDEFGHIJKLMNOPQRST
abcdefghijklmnopqrstuvwxyz
1234567890(&.,:;!?'"''-*$/)

Times Roman
ABCDEFGHIJKLMNOPQR:
abcdefghijklmnopqrstuvwxyz
1234567890(&.,:;!?'"''-*$/)

Clarendon
ABCDEFGHIJKLMNOPQRST
abcdefghijklmnopqrstuvwxy:
1234567890(&.,:;!?'"''-*$/)

11

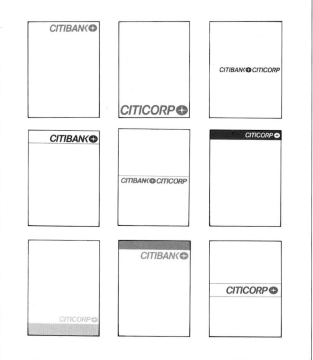

12

9

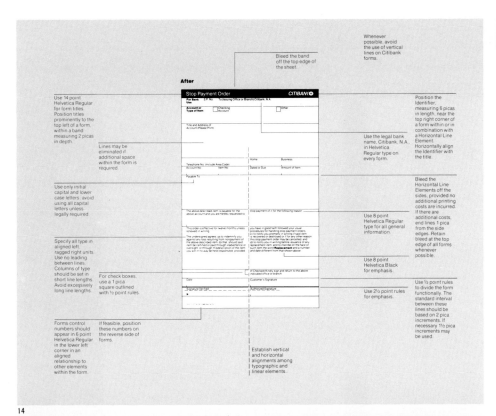

Whenever possible, avoid the use of vertical lines on Citibank forms.

Bleed the band off the top edge of the sheet.

After

Use 14 point Helvetica Regular for form titles. Position titles prominently to the top left of a form, within a band measuring 2 picas in depth.

Lines may be eliminated if additional space within the form is required.

Use only initial capital and lower case letters; avoid using all capital letters unless legally required.

Specify all type in aligned left, ragged right units. Use no leading between lines. Columns of type should be set in short line lengths. Avoid excessively long line lengths.

For check boxes, use a 1 pica square outlined with ½ point rules.

Forms control numbers should appear in 6 point Helvetica Regular in the lower left corner in an aligned relationship to other elements within the form.

If feasible, position these numbers on the reverse side of forms.

Position the Identifier, measuring 6 picas in length, near the top right corner of a form within or in combination with a Horizontal Line Element. Horizontally align the Identifier with the title.

Use the legal bank name, Citibank, N.A. in Helvetica Regular type on every form.

Bleed the Horizontal Line Elements off the sides, provided no additional printing costs are incurred. If there are additional costs, end lines 1 pica from the side edges. Retain bleed at the top edge of all forms whenever possible.

Use 8 point Helvetica Regular type for all general information.

Use 8 point Helvetica Black for emphasis.

Use ½ point rules to divide the form functionally. The standard interval between these lines should be based on 2 pica increments. If necessary 1½ pica increments may be used.

Use 2½ point rules for emphasis.

Establish vertical and horizontal alignments among typographic and linear elements.

14

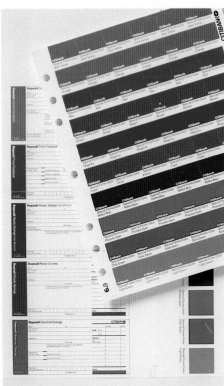

15

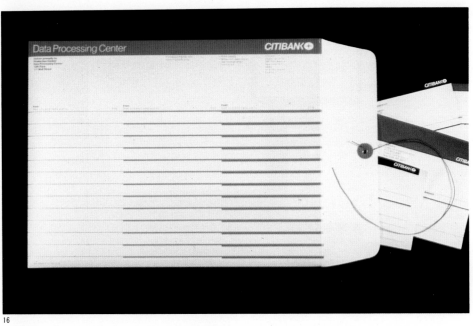

16

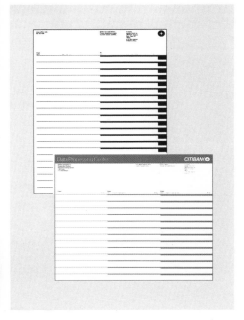

13 Various types of forms
14 Specifications for forms
   Vertical and horizontal alignments are established among typographic and linear elements.
15 Top—Special forms color control samples
   Bottom-Special forms color specifications
16 Routing envelope for in-house use
17 Specifications for routing envelopes
   Top-Large routing envelope for general use
   Bottom-Routing envelope for special use
18 Reproduction materials, Pantograph color control samples

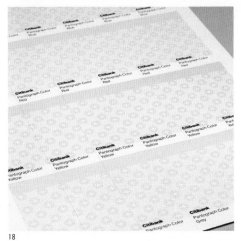

18

11

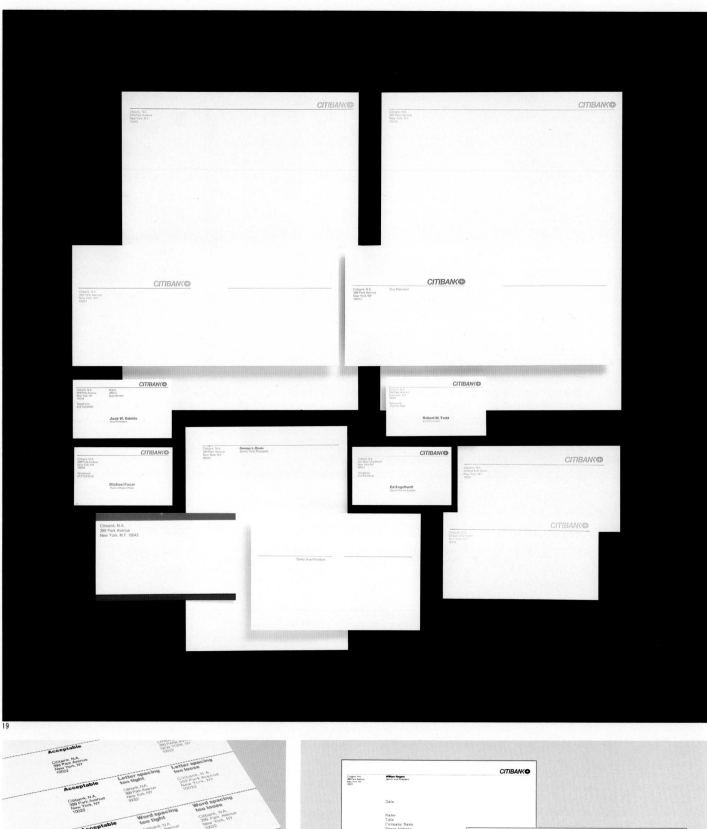

19

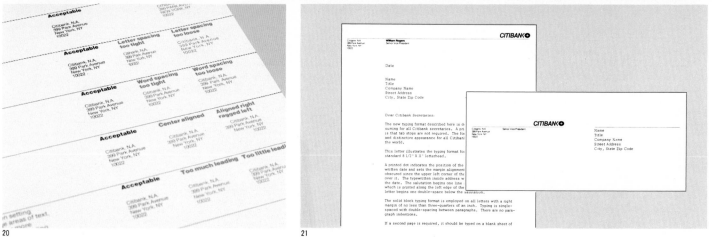

20

21

12

22

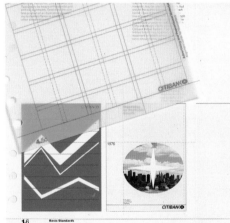

23

24

19 Stationery

Corporate Bank stationery is shown on the left; Consumer-Retail Bank stationery on the right and embossed stationery at the bottom of the page. The only color restrictions in the identity program occur on stationery items, where Citibank and Citicorp have their own individual systems.

On Citibank stationery, a blue rule is used to identify the Corporate Bank and a red rule is used for the Consumer-Retail Bank. All type printing is in gray.

20 Typographic style recommendations

Acceptable and unacceptable examples of the bank's name and address are shown.

21 Preferred typewriting formats

22·24 Catalogs and pamphlets

23 Top-Alignment guide for newsletters

Bottom-Specifications for use of illustrative materials

The symbol may be used as an outline or superimposed with a photograph. This type of use is limited to print applications only.

25

26

27

28

29

30

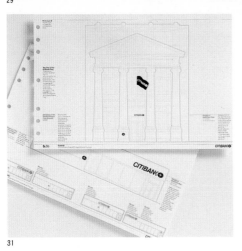

31

25 Symbol plaque applied to exterior wall
26 Identifier sign: Entrance, Citibank International Banking Center
27 Poster boards
28 Symbol applied as safety pattern on window
29 Bank name and hours applied to door
30 Signage color control samples, Color and finish specifications for primary exterior signage. Corporate Bank primary signs are matched with the predominant metal on the facade. Retail Branch Banks can use Citibank Blue, Red or Yellow. The color selected should contrast with and be compatible with the materials used on the facade.
31 Positions, sizes of primary exterior signage.

32

33

16

34

35

36

37

Citibank instituted 24 Hour Banking in 1977. Today there are over 220 such facilities in the New York metropolitan area. All centers are fully automated and may be manned, according to area demographics.

32 Entrance to 24 Hour Banking Center

33 Citicard Banking Center

34 Module Unit 24 Hour Banking Center
   This fully automated unit is located in Babylon, Long Island.

35 Automated Teller Machine

36·37 Theme Line, "The Citi Never Sleeps"
   Created as part of a retail CI campaign, this advertises the 24 Hour Banking service.

17

38

39

40

41

42

43

44

38 Customer service telephone
39 Bank interior
40 Counter Card with take-one pocket
41 Bank interior with sign advertising Direct
   Deposit of Pay into employee accounts
42 Flag with combined identifiers.
43·44 Novelties, pen and cuff link
Citicorp Center, headquarters for Citicorp, was
completed in 1978 and provides the citizens of
New York with a new dimension in urban
living. The architects, Hugh Stubbins & Associates, have designed a skyscraper that relates to
the street in a humane way.
45 Directory post
  This functional piece of outdoor furniture
  shows street directions as well as those for the
  Center itself.

46 Signage, "The Market as Citicorp Center"
   Kenneth Carbone of Gottschalk + Ash Int'l,
   New York created a sign compatible with the
   existing architecture. The bright red triangular
   panels are of perforated aluminum and reflect
   the 45° sloped roof of the Center's tower.
47 The Atrium in Citicorp Center

P&O

Headquarters: London, England
Field of Business: Conglomerate
Size of Organization:gross revenue/ £3.072 million (1981)
    number of employees/25,000
Design: Wolff Olins Limited
Year of First Implementation: 1974

P&O

1 Symbol, P&O house flag
2 P&O logotype
3 Flag "painting by numbers" guide

P&O was the main passenger and shipping line serving the British Empire in the East during the 19th and first half of the 20th century. Its luxury liners enjoyed a fine reputation for over 100 years as they served India, the Far East and Australia. Since then, there has been a dramatic change as the business has diversified and emphasis moved from passenger liners to bulk shipping, containerisation, road haulage, freight forwarding, property construction and trading. Despite this change however, the "great white liner" image, which had previously been very much an asset, remained as it was. This became the source of misunderstanding and as a result, the British design firm, Wolff Olins Limited was retained to create a new corporate identity system.

One of the elements, a stylised flag, reflects the company's trading origins. P&O supported the Royal Houses in the Spanish and Portuguese civil wars in the early 1830's. Consequently, it was able to fly the royal standards of both countries. These colors are still incorporated in the P&O house flag, the oldest symbol in the group. The new stylised flag provides a link between the non-marine activities and the sea.

4

5

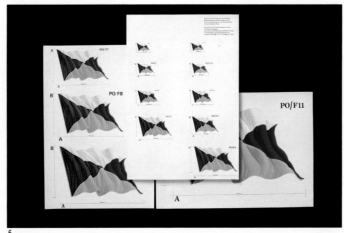

6

7

P&O Strath Services

P&O Ferries
Orkney & Shetland Services

Sea Oil Services
P&O Energy

8

P&O Bold Text
ABCDEFGHIJKLM
abcdefghijklmnopqr

P&O Bold Display
ABCDEFGHIJKLM
abcdefghijklmnopqr

9

10

Ferrymasters
P&O Unit Loads

11

12

4 CI applications broadsheet
The broadsheet shows examples suitably captioned using a combination of drawings and photographs. It includes applications for vehicles, ships, signs, clothing etc.

5 P&O CI kit

6·7 Flag specifications
The flag may be reproduced in full color or in black and white. Whenever possible, it should be reproduced in full color.

8 P&O companies, products and services are not always known by their full legal names. Shortened or familiar names become P&O logotypes when written in the P&O typefaces.

9 P&O typefaces
A range of specially drawn and related typefaces were produced to suit the wide range of application requirements. Main typefaces – P&O Bold Text: A specially designed typeface based on Plantin Bold for use in sizes up to 60 pt or 17·5mm capital letter height. P&O Bold Display: For all uses over 60pt

10~12 Logotype and flag applications

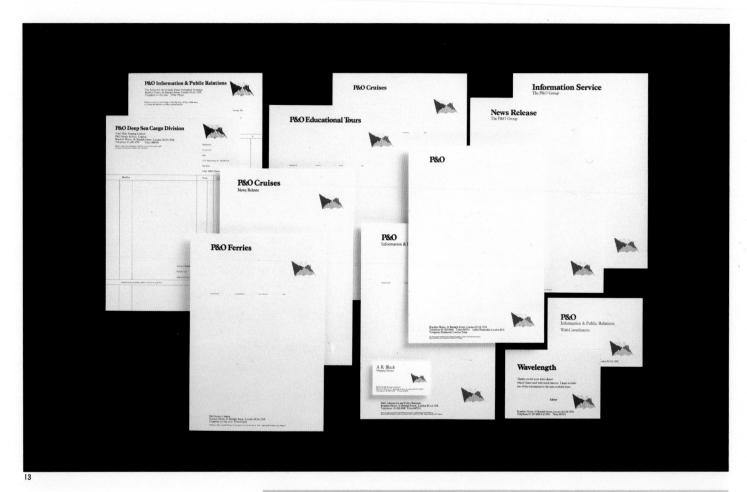

13

13 Stationery
14 Stationery specifications
Apart from the nine other typefaces, a secondary one, Plantin Light 113 is available for stationery and business forms.
15 Advertisement for P&O Ferries
16 Top-Advertisement, P&O Ferries
Bottom-Advertisement, P&O Cruising
17·18 Application of "P&O Ferries" logotype and flag to ferry

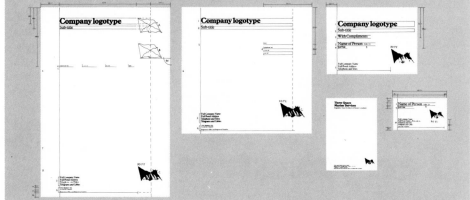

14

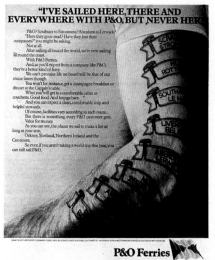

15

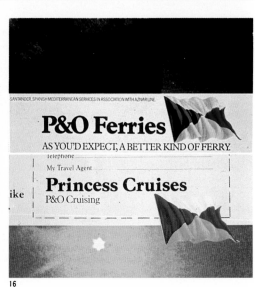

16

17

18

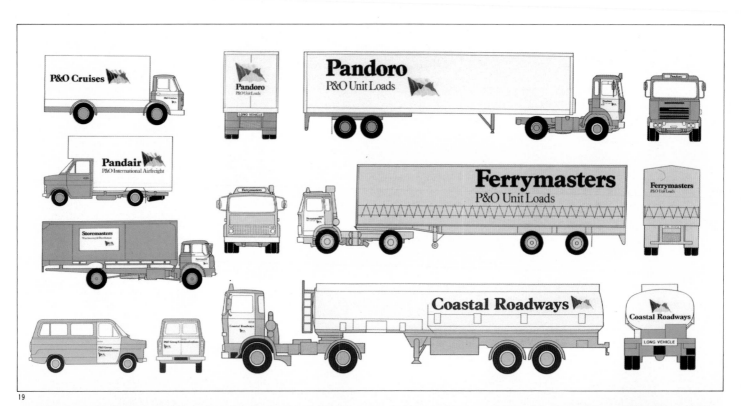

21

22

23

24

19 Marking specifications for road transport
The corporate livery scheme is based on P&O
Blue and a brilliant white. Full color flags and
black lettering are added on to white back-
grounds.
20 Flag and logotype application on double-
deck bus
21 Logotype and flag application, P&O Ferries
22 Van application, P&O Computer Services
23 Tanker application, P&O Tankmasters
24 Tanker application, Robert Armstrong P&O
Road Services

25 Truck and building sign applications
26 External sign
   Scotpac, P&O international removals
27 Building sign
28 Flag mounted on exterior wall
29 Company outlines
30 Novelty keyholder
31 Playing cards
32 Pamphlets, timetables and stickers
33 Scarf
34 P&O Falco Inc. cap
35 T shirt
36 T shirt, matchbook, playing cards and ties

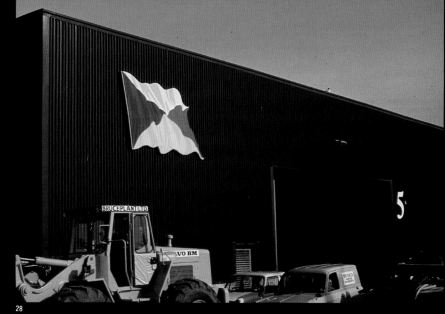

Deloitte Haskins Sells
Public Utilities Manual
Public Utilities Manual
Financial Planning Models
Illustrative Constructive Service and Internal Control Comments
Savings and Loan Associations
Accounting Practices 1978 – Small Business Investment Companies
Illustrative Items of Current Interest from Published Annual Reports
The Public Accountant in a Changing World
The Accounting Profession Responds to the Challenges by Government
Personal Tax and Financial Planning—1978
Mutual-to-Stock Conversions of S&L Associations
Accounting and Tax Considerations
Mutual-to-Stock Conversions of S&L Associations—
Services to Small and Growing Businesses
Sartoris

Headquarters: New York, U.S.A.

Field of Business: International Accounting, tax and management consulting firm

Size of Organization : number of employees/ over 25,000 worldwide

Design: Siegel & Gale (Don Ervin)

Year of First Implementation: 1979

Deloitte Haskins+Sells

In 1977, Haskins & Sells, one of America's "Big Eight", and Deloitte and Co., a prominent accounting firm in the U.K., decided to practise under the combined name of Deloitte Haskins & Sells. This had been used previously for their joint practices abroad.

For public accounting firms, the mid-seventies brought new possibilities in advertising as well as growing competition in business and recruiting. Recognizing the need for an identity program, Deloitte and Co. and Haskins and Sells engaged the New York design firm of Siegel and Gale to create a complete graphic system to convey their new identity. The image of precision and quality is communicated through a program centering on the adoption of a single name for the logotype. Stacking the names on two separate lines increases the logotype's visual impact as a unit. It also maintains the equity of both names and continuity in those areas of the world where the combined name was already in use.

Application of the program to all printed materials strengthens the firm's worldwide identity as a unified professional organization.

1 Logotype
  The logotype usually appears in a narrow block of white or a color, separated from the body copy by a rule. The plus sign was used instead of an ampersand to conform to contemporary European design practice.

2 The logotype applied to an interior wall sign

3

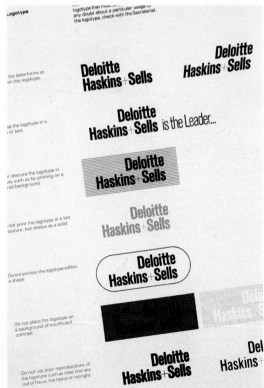

Antonio Leira Bastidas

Nieto Heffes Martínez y Cía

Livingstone Registrars Ltd

Hutchison Hull+Co

Tuncho Granados +Asociados

4

Deloitte Haskins+Sells Nederland

| × | | × |

GMBH
Management
Consultants

LTDA

Ltd.

Overseas

A.G./S.A.

AB

Limited

International

S. de R.L.

Central America

Netherlands Antilles

5

Logotype

6

Deloitte Haskins+Sells GMBH

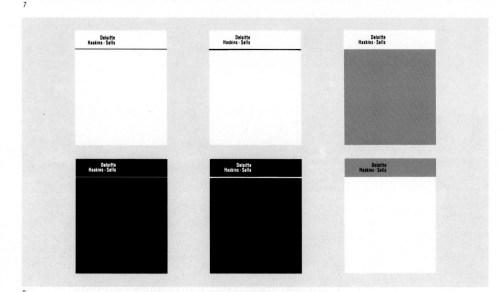

3 Communications Manual

4 Alternative logotypes

These logotypes are for firms who, for legal reasons must operate under another name, and for those firms wishing to adapt their local materials to the firm Identity System.

5 Modifiers

Some countries legally require that modifiers be used with the logotype.

6 Incorrect usage of the logotype

7·8 Identification format

The logotype together with a thin line below it form the identification format. The minimum distance from the bottom of the logotype to the line is never less than the height of a lower case letter. The preferred weight of the line is 1/2 point. PMS Warm Red is the preferred color for the line.

Particularly with publications, the appearance of a line is "created" by the edges of two adjacent blocks of different color.

9 Publication colors-uncoated

Specific PMS colors are assigned to each of the nine different subject categories.

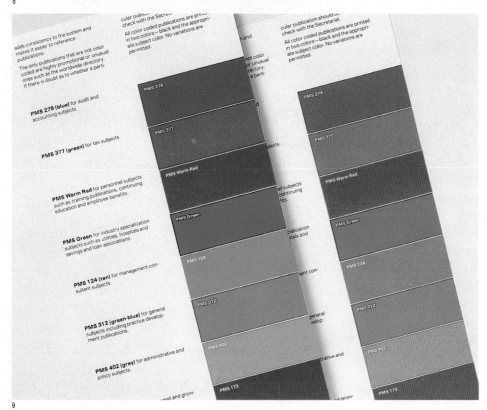

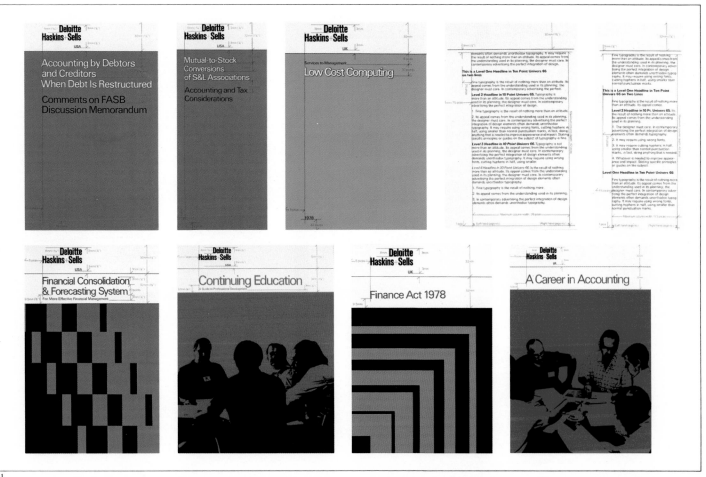

11

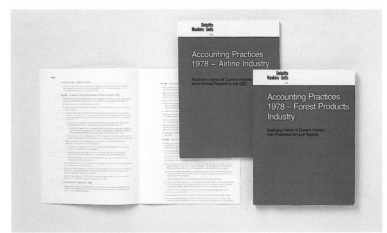

12

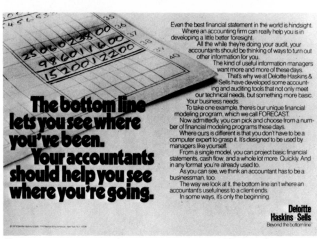

13

14

10-14 Brochures

11 Brochure cover formats
Technical publications use the logotype on a
white block, with the title appearing in black
on a solid-color cover. Promotional publications show the logotype on a white field, with
2-color art or photographs on a color coded
field. Formats for American paper sizes as well
as the standard DIN formats used in Europe
and the U.K. were created.
Cover information may include the title,
subtitle and secondary information such as a
series number.

12 Annual reports

13 Advertisement using official slogan, "Be-
yond the bottom line"

15 Stationery

16 Stationery specifications

Stationery formats also conform to both US paper sizes and DIN standards.

Mailing labels were designed for worldwide use.

17 Headquarters office, wall-mounted sign

18. Logotype applied to interior window

19 Specifications for signs

A distinctive system was developed for worldwide use. Modifiers and statements of affiliation are positioned above the red line and professional descriptions below. There are four sizes of signs; three rectangular and one square. The positioning of information on signs should never be altered. Size may be modified slightly be shortening (rectangular signs from the right side and square signs from the bottom).

20 Positioning of signs

All signs are positioned so that the red line is 152cm (5') from the finished floor.

17

18

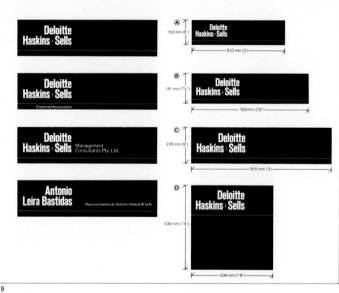

19

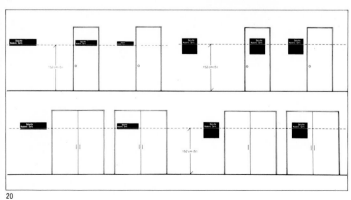

20

Watneys

Watney Mann Truman Brewers Limited

Headquarters: London, England
Field of Business: Brewers
Size of Organization: sales/£588.7 million
  number of employees/8,000
Design: Pentagram Design (John McConnell)
Year of First Implementation: 1980

1

2

3

Watneys, one of Britain's largest brewers, adopted a new attitude to its corporate identity during the 1970's. At that time, pressure from consumer groups such as CAMRA (Campaign for Real Ale) which were opposed to the large-scale production of a traditional product, resulted in changes in the market. Watneys therefore needed to produce more traditional products and market regionally to reflect local needs. The international design firm, Pentagram was appointed to advise on such a program.

Watneys has two well-established elements of identification; the red barrel symbol and a Clarendon style typeface. These were used for the logotype and pub identification but had lost value over the past fifteen years through insensitive application. Pentagram recommended that the elements be reinstated with their original quality and with variations allowing for greater flexibility in use. The new design scheme permits regional and brand identification whilst assuring continuity of image.

The new corporate identity was applied across a full range of items from stationery and promotional material to vehicles, packaging and the signing and decoration of the pubs themselves.

1 Watneys logotype with the Red Barrel symbol

2 Watneys corporate symbol

3 Watneys brand symbol

4

The Red Barrel symbol comes in two forms: a three dimensional version for signage and a two dimensional version for printed material such as stationery. The Watneys name, while retaining its traditional Clarendon typeface can be varied with five different styles of decoration. This enables a sympathetic application to all environments. The company name is contained within a ribbon motif available for use in two forms; straight and arched for use in conjunction with the red barrel.

4 Stationery
5 Watneys London regional symbol
6 Watneys Southern regional symbol
7 Promotional booklet
8 Suspended sign

5

6

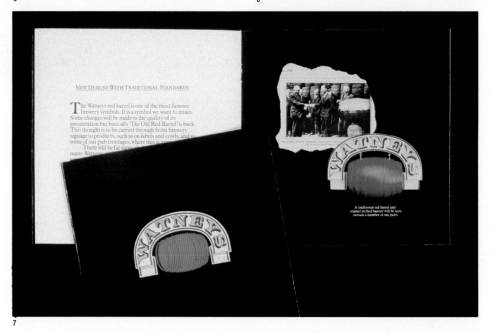

7

9

9 Pub exterior showing wall-mounted and suspended signing and completely renovated decoration with complementary color scheme.
10 Wall-mounted sign with pub name
11 Wall-mounted facilities and menu board
   The board is headed with the Watneys logotype and Red Barrel symbol and is stove-
   enamelled in corporate colors.
12 Promotional items; matches and key rings
13 Ashtray
14 Beer tap cover
15 Watneys'cart
16 Watneys Southern patch on uniform
17 Watneys' Christmas card

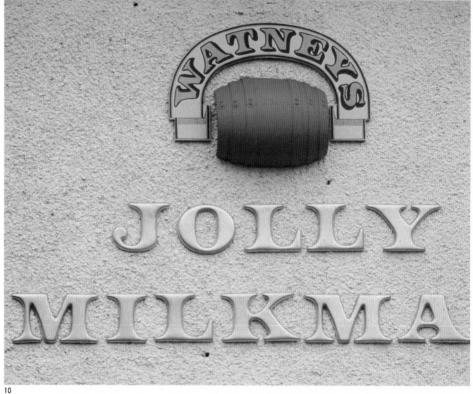

10

11

12

13

14

15

16

17

18

22

23

50

19

20

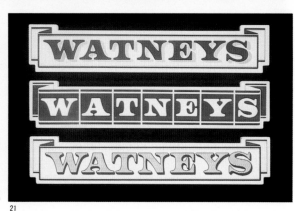

21

24

25

18-19 Vehicle livery showing use of the
Watneys name and corporate colors
20 Regional identification on vehicle livery
21 Variations on basic Watneys logotype
22 Brown Ale can and bottle labels, packaging
23 Pale Ale can and bottle labels, packaging
24 Cream Label can and bottle labels
25 Labels—Brown Ale, Pale Ale & Cream Label
The elements of the corporate identity system
were used very strongly to identify the
company's basic commodities. In the case of
branded beers, the Watneys symbol and logotype is used in a smaller form as a signature.

26 The Woodman, Wayne Anderson

27 The Montpelier, Linda Grey

28 The Seven Stars, Keren House

29

26~45 Pub signs
  Pictorial pub signs are a unique tradition in Britain. The special pub sign artists of the past have now largely disappeared to be replaced by mediocre painters of limited talent. Pentagram felt that this was a prime area for improvement and innovation and commissioned some of the best contemporary artists and editorial illustrators to inject new life into the pub signs.

29 Pole-mounted sign with illustration by Anna Pugh (The Artichoke)

30 The Free Butt, Bill Sanderson

31 The Cricketers, John Gorham

32 The Spread Eagle, Ian Miller

33 The Greyhound, Glynn Boyd Harte

34 The Horns and Two Brewers, George Hardie

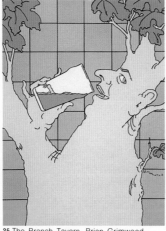

35 The Branch Tavern, Brian Grimwood

36 The Good Intent, Peter Till

37 The Fox, Bush Hollyhead

38 The Ship and Blue Ball, Dan Fern

39 The Elephant's Head, Nick Wurr

40 The George, Laurence Mynott

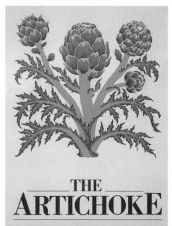

41 The Artichoke, Anna Pugh

42 The Red Lion, Mick Brownfield

43 The Wellesley, John Ireland

44 The Queen Victoria, Lars Hokanson

45 The Finish, John McConnell

53

Kenwood

Trio-Kenwood Corporation

Headquarters: Tokyo, Japan
Field of Business: Electronic equipment
Size of Organization: sales/Yen 72.5 billion
    number of employees/2,100
Design: PAOS Inc.
Year of First Implementation: 1982

1

KENWOOD

2

The TRIO-KENWOOD CORPORATION was established in 1946 and today is a well known audio specialist manufacturer. It was formerly known as TRIO in recognition of the company's three original founders. However in 1964, when the company moved into the American market, distributors there proposed that KENWOOD be used as an international brand name. Japan continued to use "TRIO" as did England, where an electrical kitchen appliance manufacturer with the name Kenwood already existed. As a result, TRIO-KENWOOD CORPORATION was introduced as the corporate name for the international market. As the company welcomed a new president in 1980, Mr. Kazuyoshi Ishizaka, a revamping of the management structure was proposed. Part of this change included the development of a new corporate identity system by PAOS, a corporate identity consulting firm in Tokyo.

The new image strategy began with a switch from using two corporate brands to only one, KENWOOD, in the international market. Design elements and a system were also developed that would always create a sense of high quality, progressiveness and smartness; the three new key image words. The new system was officially introduced in 1982.

1 KENWOOD logotype and KENWOOD triangle

2 KENWOOD corporate brand logotype
A triangle was placed above the "W" to create a focal point in the center of the rather long brand name, KENWOOD.

3 Former logotypes and symbol

TRIO
◆KENWOOD

3

57

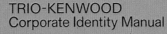

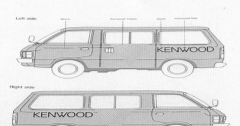
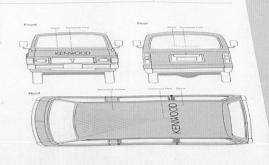

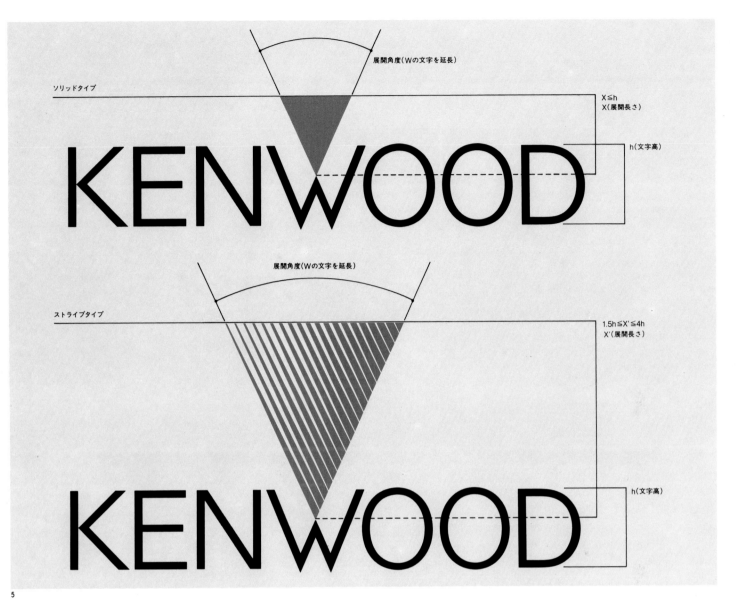

展開角度（Wの文字を延長）

ソリッドタイプ

X≦h
X（展開長さ）

h（文字高）

展開角度（Wの文字を延長）

ストライプタイプ

1.5h≦X'≦4h
X'（展開長さ）

h（文字高）

5

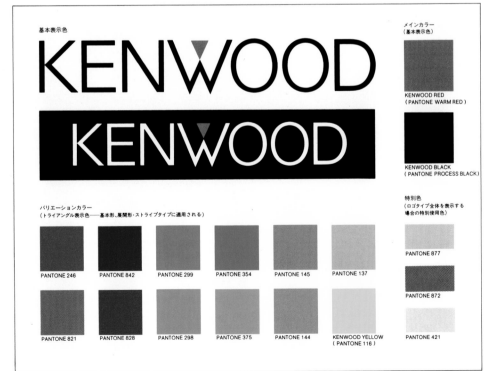

基本表示色

KENWOOD

KENWOOD

メインカラー
（基本表示色）

KENWOOD RED
（PANTONE WARM RED）

KENWOOD BLACK
（PANTONE PROCESS BLACK）

バリエーションカラー
（トライアングル表示色──基本形、展開形・ストライプタイプに適用される）

| PANTONE 246 | PANTONE 842 | PANTONE 299 | PANTONE 354 | PANTONE 145 | PANTONE 137 |
| PANTONE 821 | PANTONE 828 | PANTONE 298 | PANTONE 375 | PANTONE 144 | KENWOOD YELLOW（PANTONE 116） |

特別色
（ロゴタイプ全体を表示する
場合の特別使用色）

PANTONE 877

PANTONE 872

PANTONE 421

6

4 Corporate Identity Manual

5 Specifications for the extended logotype
The extended logotype is for promotional items such as signs, packaging and certain sales promotional materials which require an enhanced visual effect. There are two versions: one with a solid triangle which is generally used for official or corporate items and the other with a diagonally striped triangle for promotional items. The extended triangle, like that in the standard logotype maintains the same angle derived from the "W".

6 Color system for the KENWOOD logotype

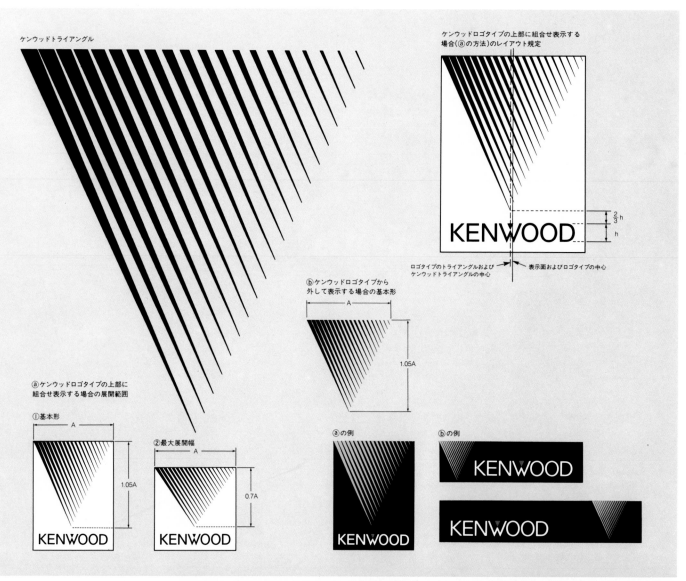

ケンウッドトライアングル

ケンウッドロゴタイプの上部に組合せ表示する
場合（ⓐの方法）のレイアウト規定

ⓑ ケンウッドロゴタイプから
外して表示する場合の基本形

ⓐ ケンウッドロゴタイプの上部に
組合せ表示する場合の展開範囲

① 基本形

② 最大展開幅

ロゴタイプのトライアングルおよび
ケンウッドトライアングルの中心

表示面およびロゴタイプの中心

ⓐの例

ⓑの例

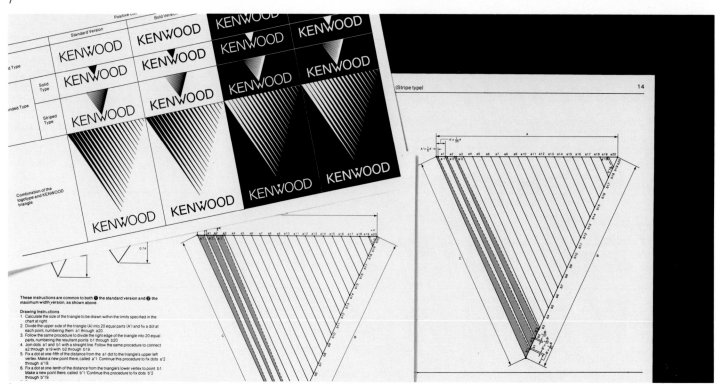

These instructions are common to both ❶ the standard version and ❷ the
maximum width version, as shown above.

Drawing Instructions

1. Calculate the size of the triangle to be drawn within the limits specified in the
   chart at right.
2. Divide the upper side of the triangle (A) into 20 equal parts (A') and fix a dot at
   each point, numbering them a1 through a20.
3. Follow the same procedure to divide the right edge of the triangle into 20 equal
   parts, numbering the resultant points b1 through b20.
4. Join dots a1 and b1 with a straight line. Follow the same procedure to connect
   a2 through a19 with b2 through b19.
5. Fix a dot at one-fifth of the distance from the a1 dot to the triangle's upper left
   vertex. Make a new point there, called a'1. Continue this procedure to fix dots a'2
   through a'19.
6. Fix a dot at one-tenth of the distance from the triangle's lower vertex to point b1.
   Make a new point there, called b'1. Continue this procedure to fix dots b'2
   through b'19.

和文社名ロゴタイプ
横組

トリオ株式会社

縦組 トリオ株式会社

英文社名ロゴタイプ

TRIO-KENWOOD CORPORATION

英文社名用タイプフェース

ABCDEFGHIJKL MNOPQRSTUV WXYZ & mb ( ) -.,

9

和文(モリサワ・ゴシック体)

中ゴシック体(BBB1)
愛伊運園岡海京区形庫佐志酢世相多知
アイウエオカキクケコサシスセソタチ

太ゴシック体(B101)
愛伊運園岡海京区形庫佐志酢世相多知
アイウエオカキクケコサシスセソタチ

見出ゴシック体(MB31)
愛伊運園岡海京区形庫佐志酢世相多知
アイウエオカキクケコサシスセソタチ

見出ゴシック体(MB101)
愛伊運園岡海京区京庫佐志酢世相多知
アイウエオカキクケコサシスセソタチ

英文(ヘルベチカ)

ライト
ABCDEFGHIJKLMNOPQRSTUV
abcdefghijklmnopq 1234567890

レギュラー
ABCDEFGHIJKLMNOPQRSTU
abcdefghijklmno 1234567890

メディウム
ABCDEFGHIJKLMNOPQRST
abcdefghijklmn 1234567890

ボールド
ABCDEFGHIJKLMNOPQR
abcdefghijkl 1234567890

10

11

12

7 KENWOOD triangle
Extension of the KENWOOD triangle, to be shown in yellow, creates a strong visual impact. The angle of extension can be varied within a set width. This systematic and flexible approach can be adapted to all products and items.

8 KENWOOD logotype usage chart, Calculation standards for the KENWOOD triangle

9 English and Japanese corporate logotypes

10 Typefaces

11 Specifications for corporate signature

12 Top-TRIO brand logotype
In Japan, England and some other commonwealth countries, the brand change from TRIO to KENWOOD on existing products will take some time. A new TRIO logotype has therefore been created to complement the new design. However this is strictly a supplementary element for use until the changeover is completed.
Bottom-Printed matter with TRIO brand logotype

13

TRIO-KENWOOD is unique in that apart from it audio products, it has three other operational divisions; communications equipment, testing instruments and records. Its ham radios and oscilloscopes are particularly well known. KENWOOD logotype applied to various products

13 (top down) FM Stereo Tuner, Stereo Integrated Amplifier, Digital Audio Disc Player
14 AM-FM Stereo Tuner
15 New High Speed Stereo Integrated Amplifier
16 Car Audio Speaker
17 Personal Transceiver

The most important aspect of the new CI system was to coordinate on a visual image level, the improvements and progress achieved by such electronic techniques as miniaturiza-

tion, enhanced effectiveness and performance of products and the emergence of digital audio technology. Consequently, by applying the new design to all products and application items, it became known in the marketplace and in the society at large, that "TRIO had changed", and was a progressive firm.

14

15

16

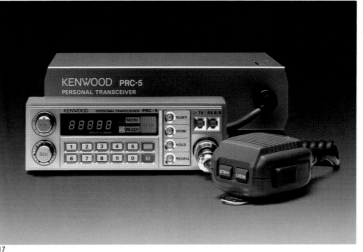

17

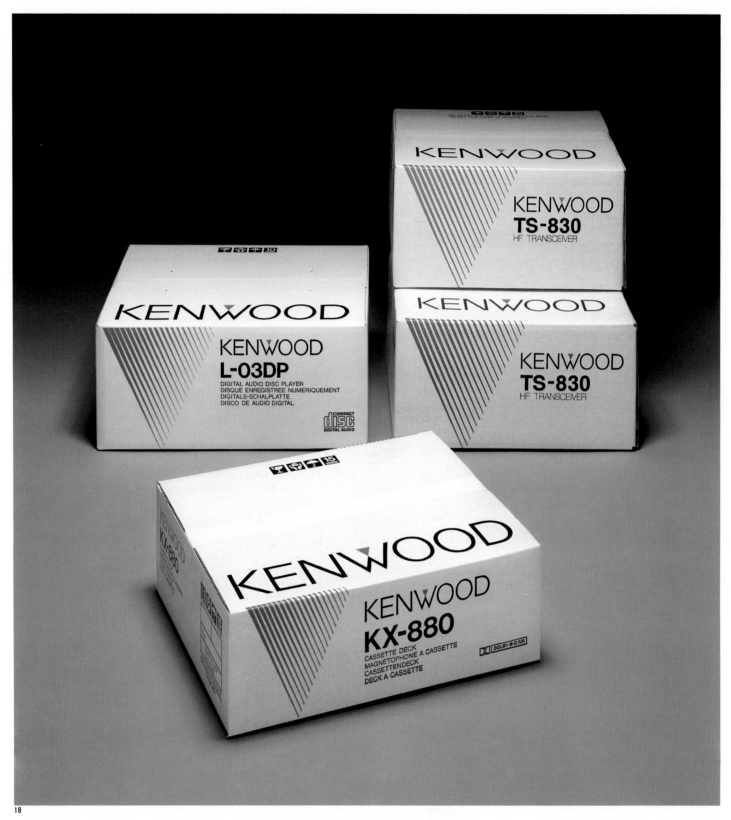

18

18 Packaging showing application of KENWOOD logotype and KENWOOD triangle

19 Packaging, communications equipment

20 Audio cassette and video tape packaging

21 Record labels

22 KENWOOD and TRIO brand headphones

23 Packaging, stereo cassette player

As the main design elements, the logotype and triangle are applied to all types of packaging to give a unified image for the company.

The triangle is extended at its upper edge and represents a condensed image of the spreading of sound. Modified stripes have also been designed and are used when a visual form of promotion is required.

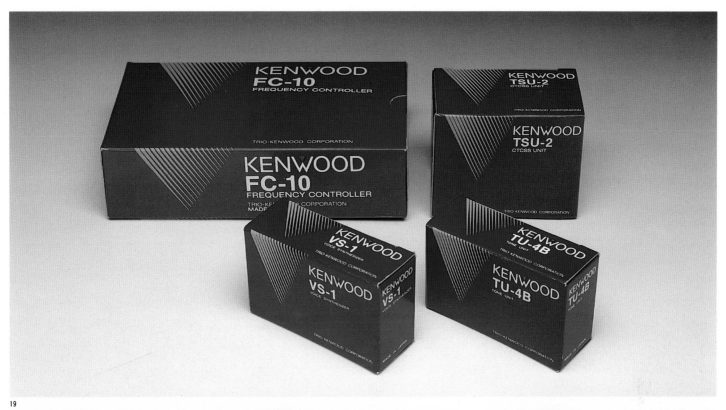

19

20

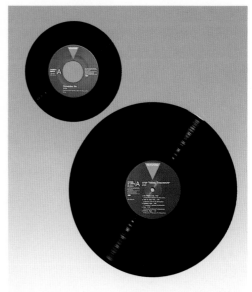

21

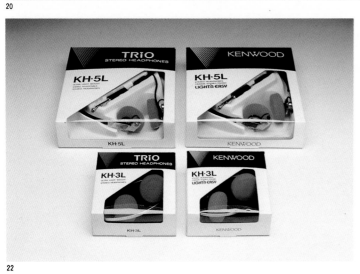

22

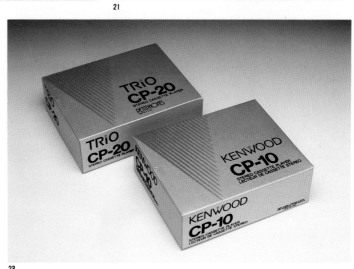

23

24

26

27

25

28

29

30

31

24·25 Factory sign, Tsuruoka, Japan

Rather than simply apply the sign to the building, the building itself has become a sign. Wall materials and the color system were adapted to suit this concept. The factory has since become a significant landmark for the area.

26 Door sign, Head Office reception area

27 Office door sign

When the logotype is applied in a vertical fashion, the base of the triangle should face an open area to help create the idea of sound spreading.

28 Projecting sign for Communications Equipment Office

29 Entrance door sign at a branch office

30·31 Neon sign

As with the factory sign, the logotype and triangle are on a black background. This helps to isolate the yellow triangle and the white logotype from the surrounding buildings and signs, making the advertisement an object of attention.

32

33

34

35

32~35 Displays at the Audio Fair held at Harumi, Tokyo in October 1982

The fair was an excellent opportunity for the promotion of the new CI system which had been announced only the month before. The display signs with the KENWOOD logotype and KENWOOD triangle on a black background were impressive examples of the company's new image.

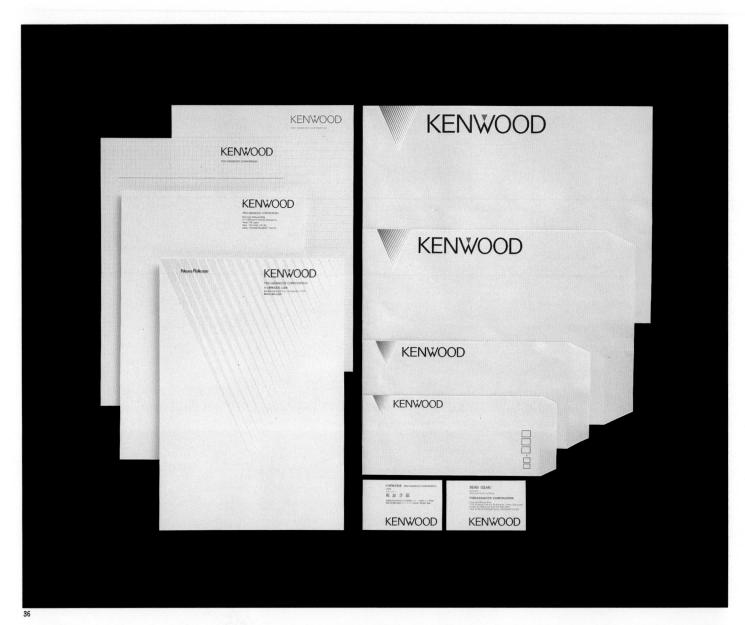

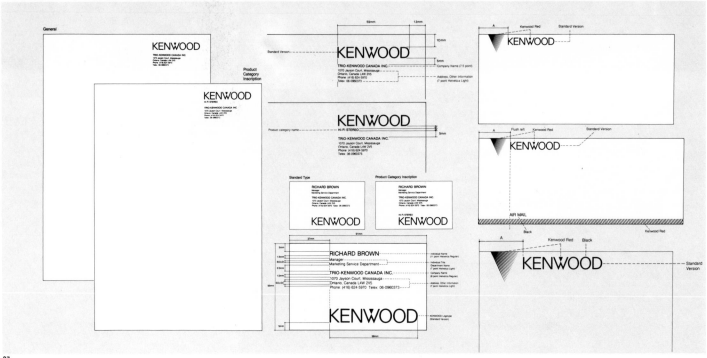

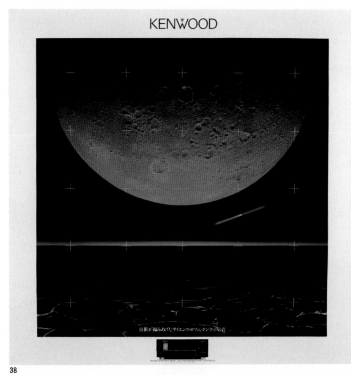

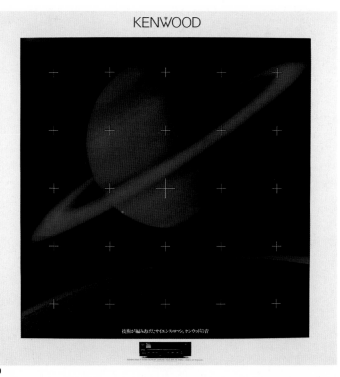

38

39

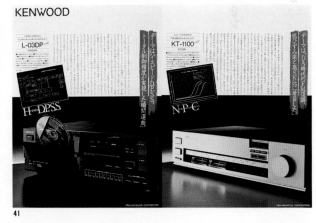

40

41

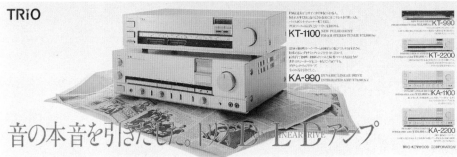

43

36 Stationery

37 Specifications for stationery

The logotype may be used alone or in combination with the triangle which is shown in KENWOOD Red. All typesetting is flush left.

38·39 Posters for audio products

40 Product catalog

41 Magazine advertisement

42 Newspaper advertisements

Top-New Year greetings and announcement of new CI system

Bottom-Digital Audio products advertisement

43 Advertisement for TRIO brand products

42

44

45

46

47

44·46·47 Vehicle markings
45 Marking specifications for vehicles
The body color is Silver Metallic. The logo-type and triangle are applied to both sides and the roof, while the logotype alone is applied to the front and back of the vehicle.
48 Catalogs for KENWOOD brand products
49 Catalog stand
50 Catalogs for TRIO brand products
51 Novelty-Car rubbish box
52 Shopping bag
The use of the triangle here gives a strong visual impact.

53 Employee badge
54 Company brochure in English
55 POP sign
56 Press kit announcing the introduction of the new CI system

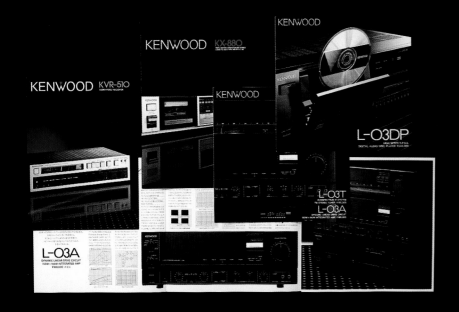

48

49

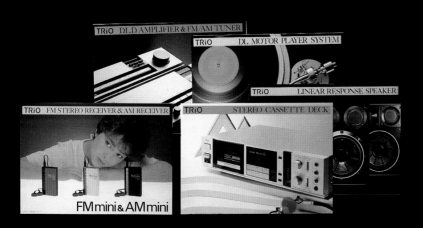

50

51

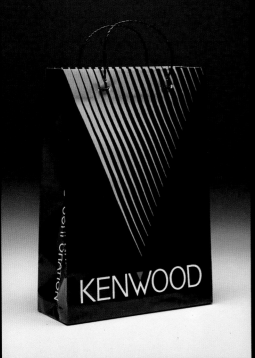

52

53

55

54

56

Cummins

Cummins Engine Company, Inc.

Headquarters: Columbus, Indiana, U.S.A.
Field of Business: Design and manufacture of
    diesel engines and component parts
Size of Organization: sales/$1.96 billion (1981)
    number of employees/22,788
Design: Paul Rand
Year of First Implementation: 1973

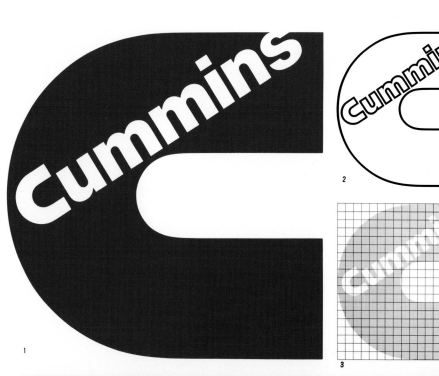

1

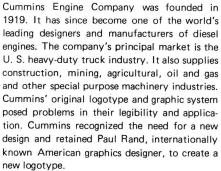

2

3

General Office

4

5

Cummins Engine Company was founded in 1919. It has since become one of the world's leading designers and manufacturers of diesel engines. The company's principal market is the U. S. heavy-duty truck industry. It also supplies construction, mining, agricultural, oil and gas and other special purpose machinery industries. Cummins' original logotype and graphic system posed problems in their legibility and application. Cummins recognized the need for a new design and retained Paul Rand, internationally known American graphics designer, to create a new logotype.

The design was tested in a variety of application systems before being officially introduced in 1973.

The company's trademark now incorporates the Cummins signature within the initial letter "C". Through this treatment, Mr. Rand has successfully eliminated the problem of handling two functionally conflicting visual elements.

1 Trademark
   The signature is composed of a specially designed C with Helvetica Bold type.
2 Outline trademark
3 Trademark construction grid
4 Trademark applied to outdoor sign
5 Former symbol applied to diesel engine oil filter

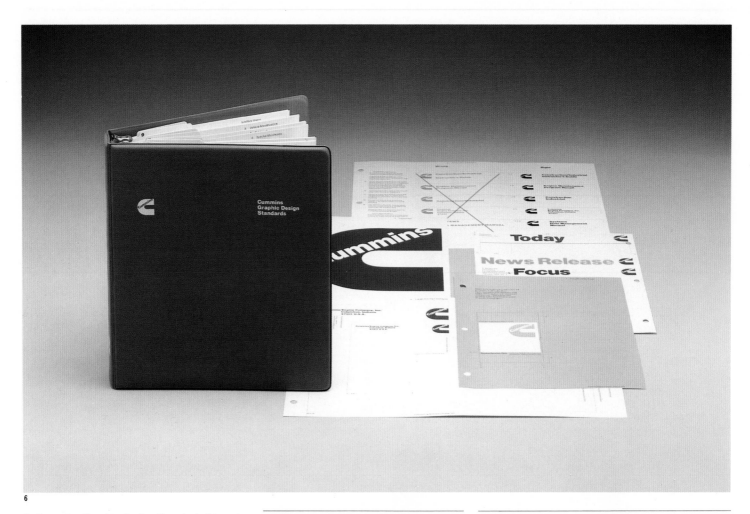

6

6 Cummins Graphic Design Standards Manual
7 Trademark application
8 Color control samples
9 Reproduction proofs for trademark and signature
10 Stationery
11 Stationery specifications
12 Specifications for advertisements, promotional literature and brochures

The usual components of an advertisement are the headline, text, a photograph or illustration, selling statement or slogan and the trademark. Brochure covers include a headline, photograph or illustration, a block of solid color and the trademark.

 Construction/Industrial Instructor's Guide

 Note on Cost Analysis

Engine Maintenance Program Recall

 Marine Engine Maintenance Instructor's Guide

Construction Industrial

 Service News

Cummins Engine Company, Inc. Columbus, Indiana 47201

 Service News

 Dealer

 Systems Data Management Manual

 Dealer

7

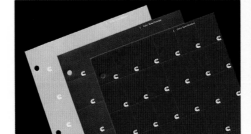

8

9

10

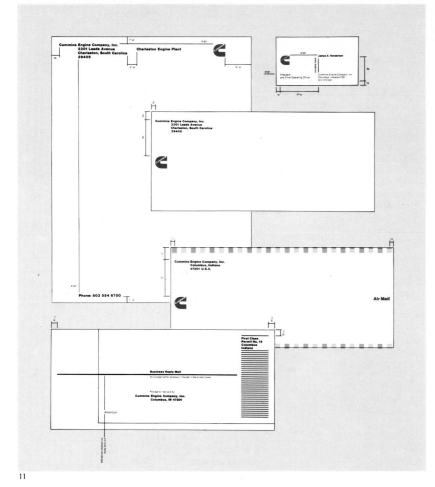

11

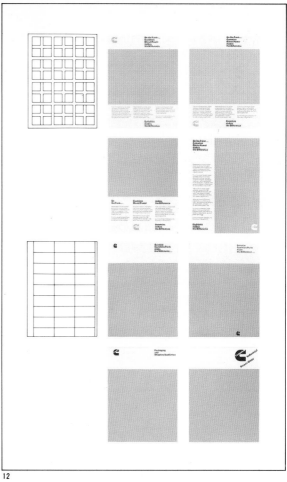

12

13

14

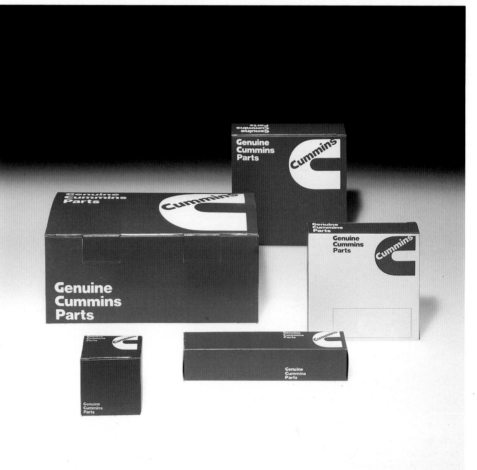

15

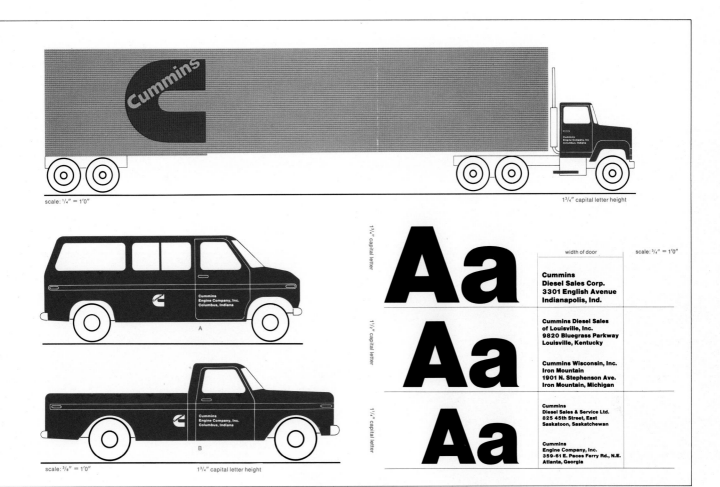

scale: 1/4" = 1'0"

1 3/4" capital letter height

A

B

scale: 3/8" = 1'0"   1 3/4" capital letter height

1 3/4" capital letter

1 1/2" capital letter

1 1/4" capital letter

width of door   scale: 3/4" = 1'0"

**Cummins
Diesel Sales Corp.
3301 English Avenue
Indianapolis, Ind.**

**Cummins Diesel Sales
of Louisville, Inc.
9820 Bluegrass Parkway
Louisville, Kentucky**

**Cummins Wisconsin, Inc.
Iron Mountain
1901 N. Stephenson Ave.
Iron Mountain, Michigan**

**Cummins
Diesel Sales & Service Ltd.
825 45th Street, East
Saskatoon, Saskatchewan**

**Cummins
Engine Company, Inc.
359-61 E. Paces Ferry Rd., N.E.
Atlanta, Georgia**

16

scale: one square equals one inch

**Cummins
Engine Company, Inc.
359-61 E. Paces Ferry Rd, N.E.
Atlanta, Georgia**

1 3/4" capital letter height

**Cummins
Engine Company, Inc.
359-61 E. Paces Ferry Rd, N.E.
Atlanta, Georgia**

1 1/2" capital letter height

**Cummins
Engine Company, Inc.
359-61 E. Paces Ferry Rd, N.E.
Atlanta, Georgia**

1 1/4" capital letter height

17

18

13 Annual reports

14 Packaging specifications
Folding cartons feature the Cummins trademark with a statement of authenticity in a bold one color scheme, Cummins blue on white stock. The basic design element, including borders, is printed on the front panel of all folding cartons. Side and end panels are imprinted with the statement of authenticity "Genuine Cummins Parts".
Parts labels also feature the trademark and statement of authenticity.

15 Various types of packaging

16·17 Specifications for vehicle identification
The trademark is aligned with the top line of the name and address.

18 Vehicle identification applied to van

19

20

21

19 Outdoor pylon sign
20 Cummins Dealer Publication Kit
21 Office manuals and guides
22 Warehouse interior
23 Trademark applied to engine
24 Big cam diesel engine
25 Cap
Novelty items
26 Carry bag
27 Lighter, matches, cuff links and keyholder
28 Paper table napkins, coasters, note paper
and pens
29 Scarf and golf balls
30 Playing cards

22

23

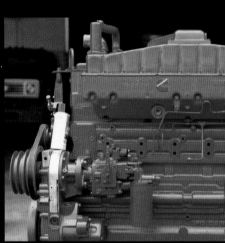

24

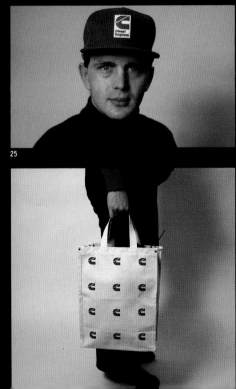

25

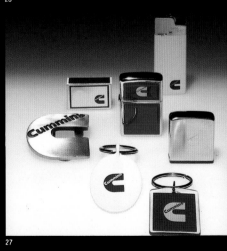

27

28

Clarks

Clarks Ltd.

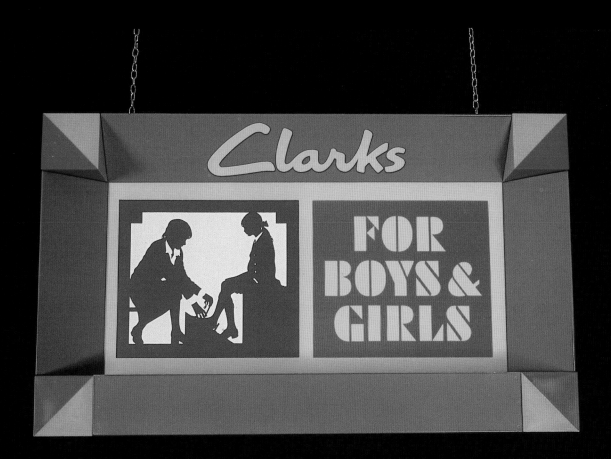

Headquarters: Somerset, England

Field of Business: Shoe manufacturing

Size of Organization: sales/Clarks Limited £140 million
    The Clarks Group £450 million
    number of employees/Clarks Limited 6,000
    The Clarks Group 20,000

Design: Pentagram Design (John McConnell)

Year of First Implementation: 1977

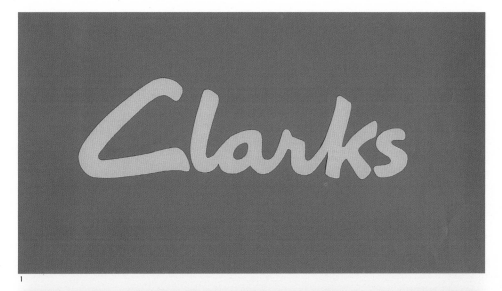

1

Founded over one hundred years ago, this English shoemakers has a long-established reputation and tradition for care and quality in children's shoes. Although the original range has now expanded to include footwear for men and women, the children's market is still predominant. In 1975, the company commissioned Pentagram, the international design firm, to improve their image by introducing a strong identity in this area.

Clarks do not own their own shoe shops, but instead distribute their goods through a network of retail outlets around the country. In addition, they provide ancillary fitting and display material to retailers, but it has never been their policy to supply heavily promotional items. It was therefore decided that a clear distinction should be made between the respective identities of the retailer and Clarks.

The basic design theme was inspired by traditional children's building blocks. These produced a variety of bold inter changeable geometric shapes that are used to link every item from the shoe boxes themselves to point-of-sale display frames and furniture.

The original Clarks signature was amended to give a clearer, chunky logotype that reads well with the rest of the scheme and bright primary colors were introduced throughout. Though Clarks' corporate color has always been green, the previous dull shade was replaced with a clearer, brighter one.

1 Clarks logotype
2 Application of logotype to shoe boxes

2

3

3 Repeat shoe box display creating a distinctive 'wall of green'.

4 Shoe box featuring logotype on lid end

5 Shoe box end label
Labels major heavily on the width fitting, which again allows use of a chunky, geometric alphabet and the same bright primary colors. The illustrations used to identify the shoe style were changed from outline to much stronger drawings.

6~8 Display and signing accessories
These accessories emphasize and promote the unique Clarks width fitting and children's foot-care story.

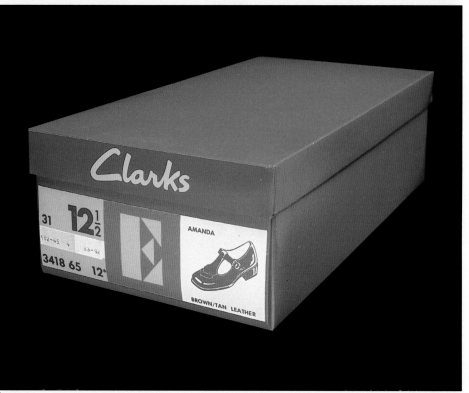

4

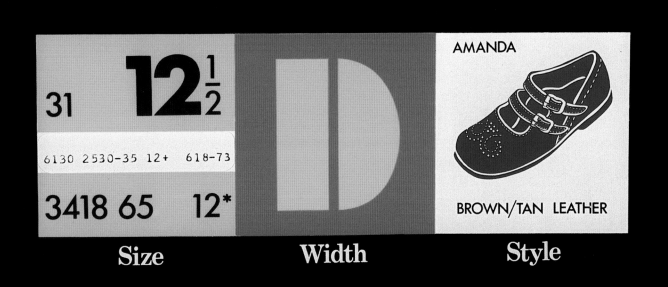

Size	Width	Style

5

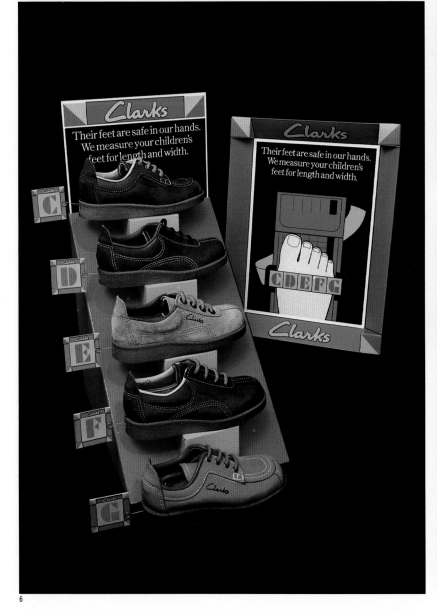

6

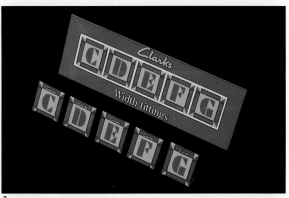

7

8

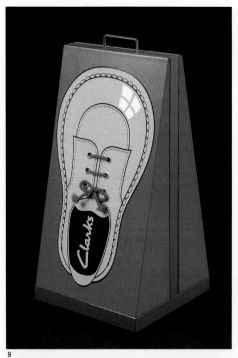

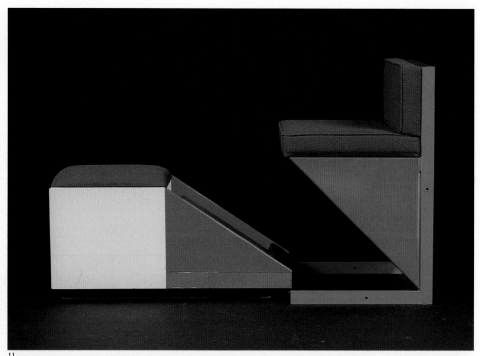

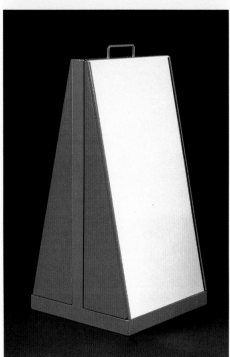

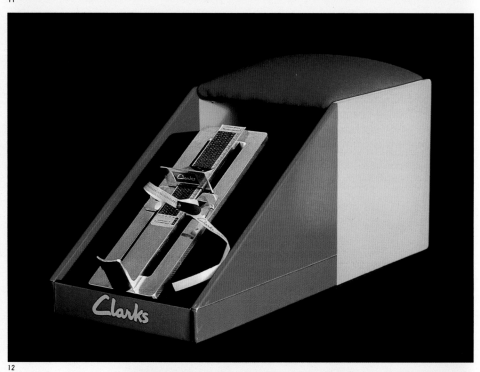

9·10 Portable floor-standing mirror, with out-
size 'how-to-tie-your-shoes' model on back
11·12 Fitting chair and stool
The wedge stool fits under the chair thus
continuing the building block idiom.
13 Staff lapel badge
14·15·17 Modular shoe display
16 Catalog of shoe styles

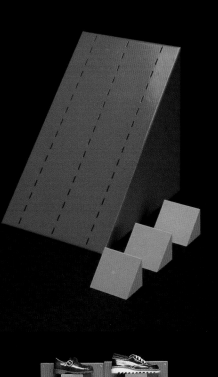

14

15

16

17

Sensible
but not
straight-
laced.

Clarks
CHILDRENS SHOES
Spring and Summer 1978

WHOSE FOOTPRINTS?

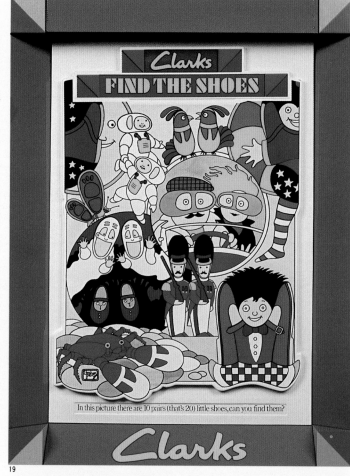

FIND THE SHOES

In this picture there are 10 pairs (that's 20) little shoes, can you find them?

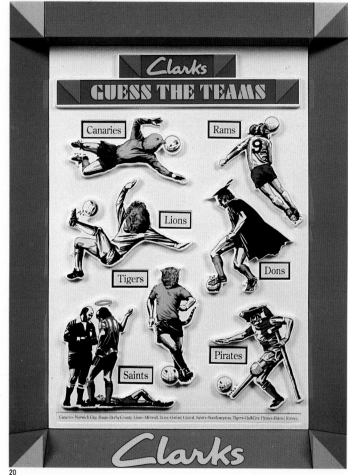

GUESS THE TEAMS

Canaries

Rams

Lions

Tigers

Dons

Saints

Pirates

Canaries-Norwich City. Rams-Derby County. Lions-Millwall. Dons-Oxford United. Saints-Southampton. Tigers-Hull City. Pirates-Bristol Rovers.

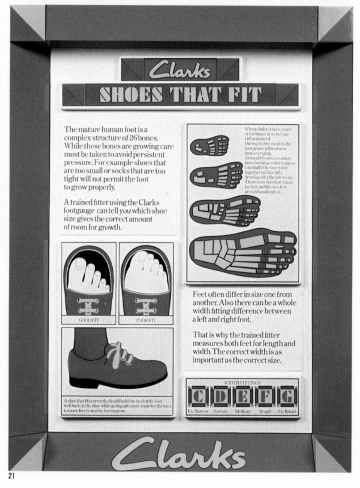

SHOES THAT FIT

The mature human foot is a complex structure of 26 bones. While these bones are growing care must be taken to avoid persistent pressure. For example shoes that are too small or socks that are too tight will not permit the foot to grow properly.

A trained fitter using the Clarks footgauge can tell you which shoe size gives the correct amount of room for growth.

When a baby is born, many of the bones in its feet are still unformed. During its first months the foot grows without new bones forming. Around 8 years, secondary bone forming centres appear. Gradually the bones fuse together and are fully developed by the late teens. There is no standard shape for feet and the two feet are seldom identical.

Feet often differ in size one from another. Also there can be a whole width fitting difference between a left and right foot.

That is why the trained fitter measures both feet for length and width. The correct width is as important as the correct size.

GOOD FIT

POOR FIT

A shoe that fits correctly should hold the heel of the foot well back in the shoe while giving adequate room for the toes to move freely and the foot to grow.

WIDTH FITTINGS

C D E F G

Ex. Narrow   Narrow   Medium   Broad   Ex. Broad

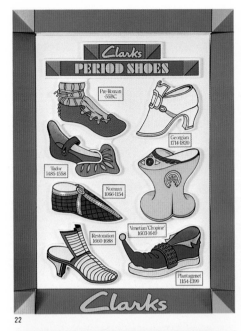

22

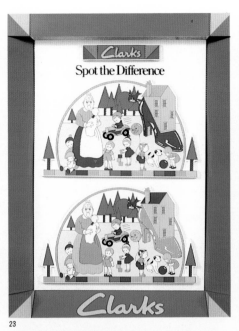

23

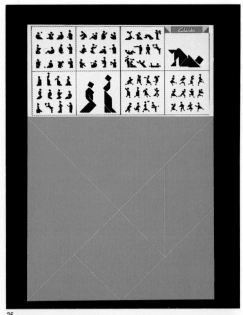

26

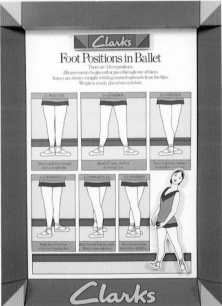

24

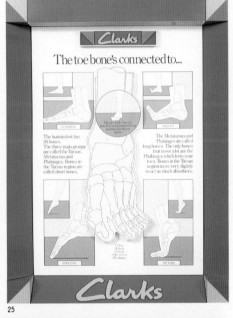

25

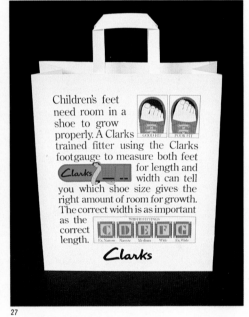

27

18~25 Display panels
These decorative and amusing panels fit frames in Clarks green with corner block detail. Aimed at specific audiences (toddlers, boys, girls and parents) the panels are based on the theme of feet or shoes, though they are not heavily promotional.

26 Tangram puzzle, give-away for children

27 Carrier bag

28 Promotional give-away booklets

28

30

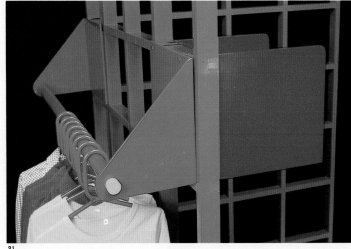

31

32

33

Following the success of the children's shoes
design scheme, the company launched a range
of children's clothes. This required a new but
related identity. The amended Clarks signature
logotype was this time applied to a buttoned
gingham pocket for the symbol. The bright,
primary colors were also retained.

Included in the program were labels, carriers,
promotional material and signs as well as a full
range of furniture and display fittings

29 Symbol and display system
 The basic grid display system, in Clarks green,
 was designed for flexible assembly into a
 variety of combinations and layouts.

30 Two variations of the display system
31 Optional display fitting
 A range of optional display fittings and
 accessories are available for use with the basic
 grid system. These allow for racking and
 hanging as desired.
32 Clothes labels
33 Carrier bag

The Citizens National Bank

The Citizens National Bank

Headquarters: Seoul, Korea

Field of Business: Banking

Size of Organization: total assets/
    Won 2,783,169 million
    number of employees/8,953

Design: Young Jae Cho, Young Jae Cho
    CI Research Group

Year of First Implementation: 1980

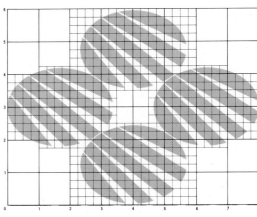

The Citizens National Bank (CNB), was established in 1963 as a government owned bank under "The CNB Act". As the name implies, CNB concentrates on serving the general public and small-scale enterprises. With the appointment of Mr. Byoung Soon Song as President in 1980, the bank began to push ahead with new management policies such as mechanization, development of new product lines and employee training. At the same time Korea's number one designer Mr. Young Jae Cho was retained to develop a CI system that would portray the bank's new image.

The system's basic concepts were "friendliness" for a people's bank and "progressiveness" to reflect the bank's positive attempts to adapt to a changing management environment.

Two years after the system's introduction, total deposits had increased rapidly from 1·1 trillion to 2·6 trillion Won, making CNB Korea's largest bank, in terms of deposits.

1·2 Corporate symbol (four-leaved clover) and its grid scale

3 Symbol applied to corporate flag

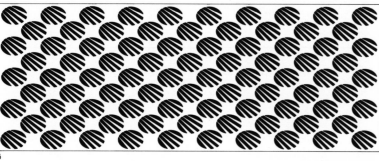

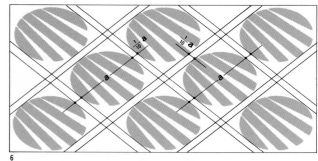

4 CNB's CI manual
The manual comprises two volumes: the "Basic Design System" and the "Application Design System".

5 Symbol pattern

6 Guidelines for construction of pattern

7 Corporate logotype (horizontal, vertical and English versions) and signature system
The logotype has been neatly designed to make the symbol appear more prominent.

8 Corporate colors
Blue is the main color with orange and green used as sub-colors. Black, silver and gold are also available for restricted use.

9 Signature specifications
Apart from symbol and logotype specifications, there are also specifications for signatures including addresses.

국민은행

The Citizens National Bank

國民銀行

국민은행

國民銀行

국민은행

國民銀行

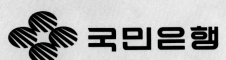

The Citizens National Bank

국민은행

國民銀行

국민
은행

國民
銀行

7

8

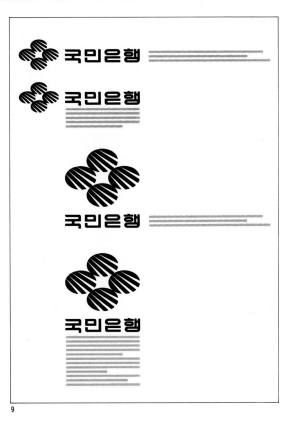

9

101

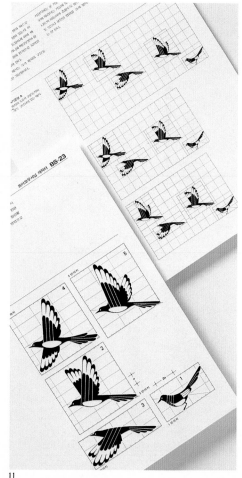

10

11

10 CNB's "character"

This character symbolizes the "friendly" image of the bank. Along with the symbol and logotype, it is one of the important basic design elements.

The magpie is considered a lucky bird and is believed to bring good news. It is the favourite bird of the Korean people.

There are five variations of the bird in flight. These can be combined to express "friendliness" and the "dynamic" image of the corporation.

11 Specifications for application of the character on various items

12 Specified typeface

Medium and bold versions are available.

13 CNB's head office

당	좌	보	통	저	축	정	기	특	별
가	계	예	금	수	납	대	출	외	환
은	행	장	실	이	사	기	획	조	사
업	무	부	신	용	서	무	시	공	과
전	자	계	산	국	제	관	리	지	점

당	좌	보	통	저	축	정	기	특	별
가	계	예	금	수	납	대	출	외	환
은	행	장	실	이	사	기	획	조	사
업	무	부	신	용	서	무	시	공	과
전	자	계	산	국	제	관	리	지	점

12

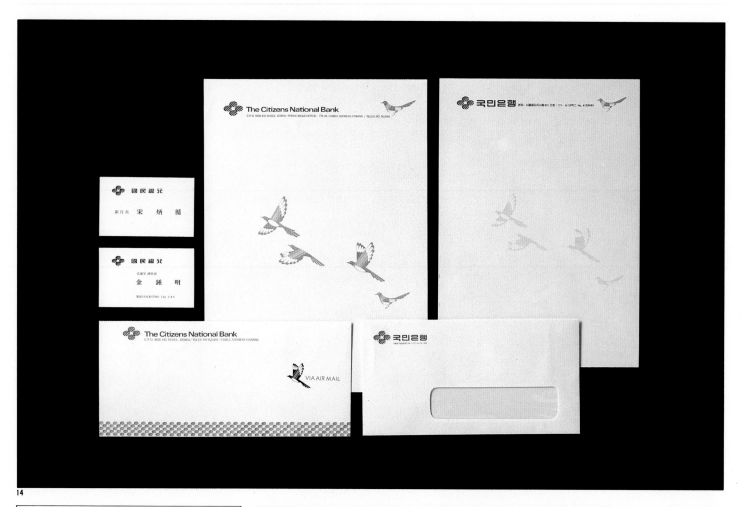

14

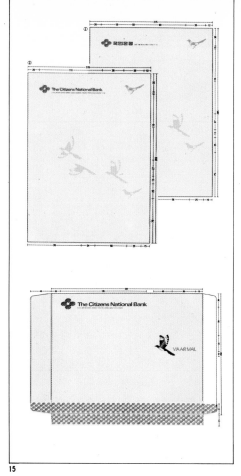

15

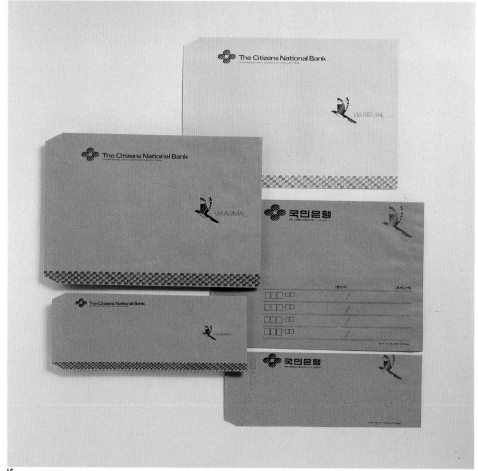

16

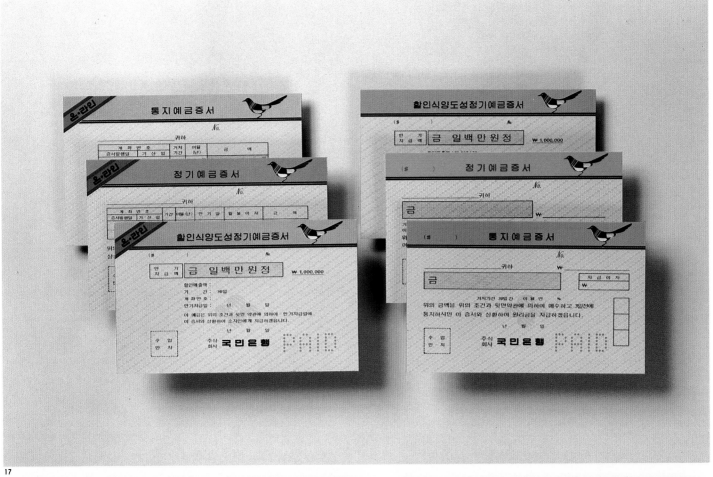

17

18

19

20

14·16 Stationery
15 Top-Specifications for letterheads for overseas and domestic use
Bottom-Specifications for airmail envelopes
for overseas use
17 Certificates of deposit
Certificates with a diagonal stripe on the
upper left hand corner are for on-line use.
18 Bankbooks
19 Bankbooks and certificates
20 Symbol pattern applied to paper used for
wrapping cash
The symbol pattern and character are used as
elements to symbolize the bank.

21

22

국민은행
중부지점
The Citizens National Bank

23

24

25

26

27

28

29

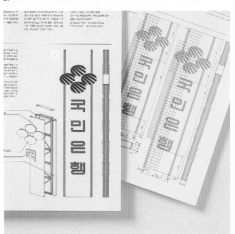

30

21 Symbol, logotype and character applied to parapet of head office
22 Pole sign
23 Parapet signage
24 Symbol, logotype and character applied to shutter
25 Major sign
26 Symbol, logotype and character applied to windows
27 Counter signs
28 Information board
29 Cash dispenser
30 Specifications for design and production of signs

31

32

33

31 Employee commuter bus
32 Van for delivery of cash
33 Truck
34 Credit cards and signs
35 Novelty money box
36 Gift-packed cigarettes, momento for CNB's
   eighteenth anniversary
37 Uniforms
38 Badge for female employees
39 Ashtray
40 left-Employee name tags
   right-Plastic numbered waiting cards
41 Pamphlet case
42 Pamphlets
43 Annual reports

4

7

35

36

38

39

40

41

Washington Zoo

National Zoological Park, Smithsonian Institution, Washington, D.C.

National Zoological Park, Smithsonian
   Institution
Location: Washington, D.C., U.S.A.
Size of Organization: total animal population/2,884
   area/165 usable acres, visitors/3.5 million per year
   employees/294 full-time,100 volunteers
Design: Wyman & Cannan Ltd., National Zoo
   Office of Graphics and Exhibits (Robert Mulcahy)
Year of First Implementation: 1977

1

2

3

4

5

6

The graphics program is a diverse one. Yet it is unified by the extraordinary use of the "O" from the specially designed soft square typeface. The highly adaptable "O" forms the frame for animal pictographs and is also a major element of totems, map stands, kiosks etc. Mr. Mulcahy and his design team continually adapt the program to suit the varying animal population by introducing changes in keeping with the original concept.

1 Logotype applied to entrance sign
2·3 Logotype variations
4~6 Zoo symbol variations
  The new symbol of a bald eagle, America's national bird, feeding its chick, represents the continuation and renewal of species.

The Smithsonian Institution's National Zoological Park, located in Washington, D.C., U.S.A., presents a unique example of environmental graphics. Results of a visitor survey in 1974 revealed the need for a concise Zoo identity. Consequently, the National Endowment for the Arts proposed Master Architectural and Graphic Plans. The latter saw the hiring of Robert E. Mulcahy as art director in 1974, who along with the then New York design firm of Wyman and Cannan created an original graphics program for the Zoo.

7

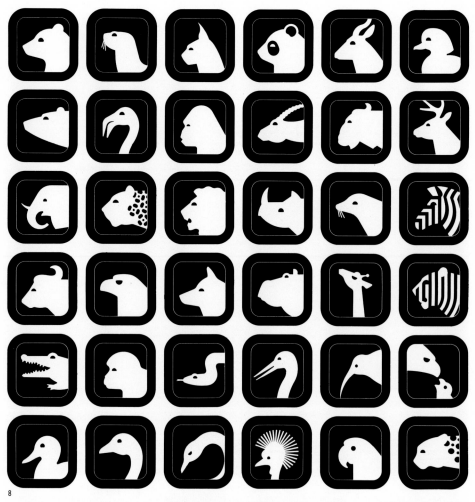

8

Design work for the Zoo's directional trail system formed the basis for the design program. Each trail begins and ends on Olmsted Walk, the Zoo's main thoroughfare named after the original planner, Frederick Law Olmsted. Totems designate the color-coded trails which are categorized by a major animal exhibit. The totems feature pictographs of the theme animal in the center with pictographs of other major animal exhibits above. The first of the lower four panels defines in copy and symbols the animal exhibits on the trail, the time it takes to walk the trail and the distance. The second panel shows the Zoo map, the third, the services available on the trail and the fourth, the tracks of the theme animal which are placed at intervals along the trail.

7 Six trail identification pictographs
8 Animal pictographs
9 Zoo typeface & soft square construction grid
10 Current Zoo map
11 Lower entrance starting map, totem, Olmsted Walk

ABCDEFGHIJK LMNOPQRSTU VWXYZ

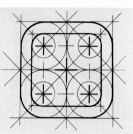

9

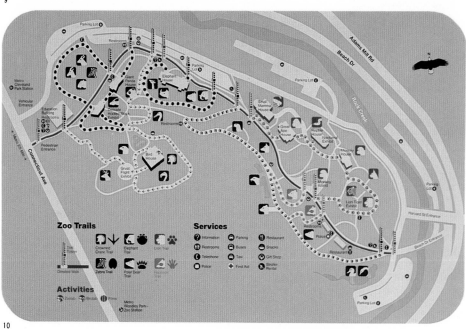

10

12

13

14

17

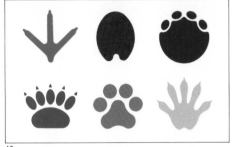

18

As of March 1983, there are six Zoo trails. The trails are developed to meet the needs of the everchanging collection of animals.

12 Crowned Crane Trail
13 Zebra Trail
14 Elephant Trail
15 Polar Bear Trail
16 Lion Trail
17 Raccoon Trail
18 Footprints

15

16

19

20

21

22

23

24

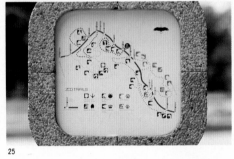

25

26

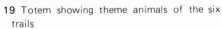

27

19 Totem showing theme animals of the six
trails
20 Totem for Lion Trail
21 Directory sign for Olmsted Walk, red stripe,
and services at the park
22 Zebra footprints
The trails are imaginatively marked with a
series of stylized animal footprints. These are
strategically placed so as to arouse the curiosi-
ty of visiting children.
23 Polar bear footprints

24·25 Zoo map
The typeface used on maps and totems is now
being changed from the soft square to Helvetica for increased legibility.
26 Food Shop banners
27 Zoo symbol banners

28

29

There are several species of animals in this exhibit.

These silhouette drawings will help you to identify them.

Bongo
Tragelaphus eurycerus

Dorcas Gazelle
Gazella dorcas

30

Atlas Lion
Panthera leo leo

León Del Atlas

Range	Now extinct in the wild. It survives only in captivity. It once lived from northern Libya west to Morocco.	Especie en peligro de extinción; existe solamente en cautiverio. En un tiempo habitó en el norte de Libia hacia el oeste de Marruecos.
Habitat	Included open mountain woodland and flatter coastal plains.	Habitó en bosques montañosos rasos y llanos costeros más planos.
Natural Diet	Included hoofstock, such as Atlas gazelles and Barbary stags.	Incluyó animales ungulados tales como la gaceta del Atlas y el ciervo de Berbería.
Reproduction	Two to four young.	De dos a cuatro crías.
Social Structure	Traveled alone, in pairs, or as mother with cubs. Not thought to be a "pride" lion, unlike other African subspecies.	Viajó solo, en parejas, y las hembras con sus crías también viajaron juntas. No se piensa que viajó en manadas, como otras sub-especies africanas.

31

HORNS OR ANTLERS?

32

Asiatic Elephant
Elephas maximus

33

34

35

36

37

28 Exhibit sign
All information copy is in Helvetica.
29 Exhibit sign
30 Bilingual exhibit signs (English & Spanish)
31 Display case
32 Information panel
33 Indoor exhibit
34 Symbol applied to doors of Education Bldg.
35 Zoo identification traffic sign
36 Speed limit sign
37 Traffic sign system with interchangeable signs
38 Ape House—Information/Education

38

40

41

39

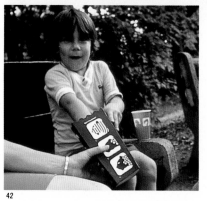

42

43

44

39 Crowned Crane pictogram on bus window
   reflected on bus seats
40 Zoo bus
41 Pictograms applied to cups
42 Popcorn container
43·44 Zoo cup
45 Uniform with Zoo symbol patch
46 Advertisement, subway station
47 Zoo poster
48·49 Advertisements for subway and buses
50 Christmas card with pictograms
51 Christmas card with animal footprints
52 Information brochures
53 Zoo stationery
54 Annual Reports

45

National Zoo **Reptile House**

on metro red line

National Zoological Park·Smithsonian Institution

46

**National Zoo
and Aquarium Month**
June 1983

47

Metro Red Line
to the National Zoo

National Zoological Park·Smithsonian Institution

48

National Zoo
Reptile House

On Metro Red Line

National Zoological Park·Smithsonian Institution

49

Symbolically Speaking

National Zoological Park·Smithsonian Institution
Peace ·1978

50

Tiger **Bear** **Panda**

52

Physical Features

Scientific Classification

Reproduction and Cubs

Peace

National Zoological Park · Smithsonian Institution · 1979

51

53

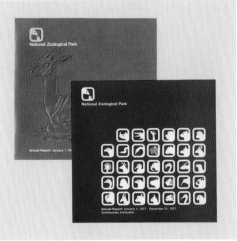

54

123

ACKNOWLEDGEMENTS

*We would like to express our gratitude to those people
who have kindly given us their assistance.*

Citibank, N.A.
Jack W. Odette (Vice President, Communication Design)
Michael Focar (Public Affairs Officer)
John B. Batt (Senior Public Affairs Officer)

Anspach Grossman Portugal, Inc.
Eugene J. Grossman (Principal)

Gottschalk & Ash Int'l, New York
Kenneth Carbone (Principal)

P & O Limited
Stephen Rabson (Group Librarian, P & O
Information and Public Relations)

Wolff Olins Limited
Wally Olins (Principal)
Barbara J. Lewis
Lisa Groocock

Siegel & Gale
Alan Siegel (President)
Barbara de Groot (Vice President)

Pentagram Design Limited, London
John McConnell
Jane Killin (Archivist)

Pentagram Design, New York
Colin Forbes
Julie Freundlich (Archivist)

Trio-Kenwood Corporation
Takayuki Itakura (Manager, Public Relations Department)
Osamu Hongo (Corporate Design Department)
Yoshiyuki Takagi (Corporate Design Department)

Cummins Engine Company, Inc.
Randall Tucker (Director, Public Relations)
Ann C. Smith (Manager, Public Information)

Paul Rand, Inc.
Paul Rand

The Citizens National Bank
Byoung Soon Song (President and Chairman of the
Board of Directors)
Jong Myoung Kim (Manager, Office for Public Relations)
Young Ki Joo (Manager, Yeo—ui—do Branch)

The Young Jae Cho CI Research Group
Young Jae Cho

**National Zoological Park, Smithsonian
Institution**
Washington, D.C.
Robert Mulcahy (Director, Office of Graphics and
Exhibits)

Lance Wyman Ltd.
Lance Wyman (President)

Bill Cannan & Co.
Bill Cannan (President)

THE AUTHORS

CoCoMAS Committee Director

Motoo Nakanishi

Born in 1938, Kobe
Kuwazawa Design Institute, Living
Design Course/Waseda Univ. (MA
in Fine Arts)
Publications: "Design Policy—A
Study on Corporate Image"
Coauthor (Bijutsu Shuppansha,
1964), "DECOMAS—Design
Coordination as A Management
Strategy" (Sanseido, 1971)
President, PAOS Inc.
Consultant: Corporate
communications and corporate
identity programs for Mazda,
Sekisui, Daiei, Koiwai, Matsuya, à
table Matsuya, Juchheim, Kirin
Beer, Mitsui Real Estate, Bridge-
stone Tire, Kanagawa Prefecture.,
Trio-Kenwood and others.

Editing and writing staff

Takao Sago

Born in 1947, Nanzan Univ. (BA in
German Language and Literature)
Sony Corp., Overseas Data Service
Co., Ltd., PAOS Inc. Coordinator,
corporate identification programs for
Nippon Shinpan and for the
development of the Toshiba Store
design system, Kanagawa Prefecture
and others.
Coordinator, The CoCoMAS
Committee.

Michelle K. Vass

Born in 1960, Brisbane, Australia
University of Queensland/Keio Univ./
ISS Inc. Simultaneous Interpreting
Course PAOS Inc.